A story of transformation

By Michelle Mapplebeck

This is my story.

I am writing this book, to share my story with you, about my life and my experiences. My ups and downs, my highs and lows, the good, bad and the ugly.

As I look back over my life, I see how my life has changed and how life choices have majorly impacted my life.

I want to share my story with you, to share and to encourage you in your own life journey. As we all know life can be very difficult and hard at times and other times we can be on top of the clouds.

As we begin, I pray for God to meet you where you are and that His Holy Spirit will speak deep down into your heart. Just as He has for me many times before.

One more thing……..enjoy.

Contents

First Published by Michelle Mapplebeck 2020
Typeset by Oxford eBooks.

Chapter 1. In the beginning
Where it all began

Let's begin, so I was born in a small town called Rugby, in Warwickshire. Yes, where the game of Rugby began. William Webb Ellis first ran with the ball while playing football, inventing the game of Rugby.

I was born at St Cross hospital in Rugby, on 22nd March 1984. We lived on Southbrook Road, a beautiful place to grow up. We were very blessed. We had a park over the road, it had a brook with fields and fields to play in and explore. It was lovely.

I lived with my mum, my sisters and brother. I have two older sisters and one brother. I was the youngest of the four. My mum and dad's marriage broke down not long after I was born, so dad left when I was a baby.

We didn't really see much of him growing up. Sometimes he would pop in and out, most of the time he wasn't there.

Dad later moved away.

My older brother and sister moved away to start their own lives. So it was just me, my sister and my mum at home. Me and my sister were very close, we still are.

We had a lot of neighbour's that had children the same age as us. So it was fun growing up, we played games on the field. Rounders being one of my favourites. Me and my sister would spend hours on our bikes, out and about making dens. I loved my dolls, Barbie and especially my Polly pockets. I would spend hours playing with my toys. Sometimes I would tell mum, I had a migraine so I could stay home and play. I was a right girly girl and loved it. I loved animals. We had hamsters, when we were growing up. Later we mated them, ending up with 9 babies. It was amazing watching them grow and develop. I also went horse riding in my teenage years but it was so expensive, I had to stop. I could have seen me being a horse girl, being outside, riding, the freedom. I would have loved that.

As we got older our bikes were our thing, we would go off for hours and hours. It was great fun, we also had skates, we would go off to roller discos at the sport centre. I would play for hours in the garden roller skating about.

As I went to high school things changed, I changed, not all for the better.

My friends were not quite like me, they would wear make-up and were interested in boys. I was not really bothered, but eventually it started rubbing off on me.

I also started smoking, eventually this led on to other things. Things weren't always great at home. My sister being a teenager too, started getting in with the wrong crowd. Her and mum would fight and argue, I found this quite hard as always felt I was in the middle.

I started smoking drugs at school and home. One day my friend took me to where she used to baby sit. Me and her mum hit it off straight away before I knew I was hanging around with them. Going out partying at the weekends, then school in the week. My sister would do my hair and make-up, so I would get into the club.

I did love going out and meeting new people. My sister also took me up town a few times. After a while this lifestyle caught up with me. I remember being very angry.

I would argue with my teachers at school. I used to skip school a lot in year 10. I tried hard in year 11, to get some grades and work hard. I did, I was getting on well but I didn't get on with my art teacher at all. I don't think she liked me, causing arguments, mostly me arguing with her. This eventually led to me being kicked out of school and not allowed back. Only to do my GCSEs, I was gutted. I had tried so hard all for nothing. Still even with this mighty blow life carried on.

I remember one evening, I had been out and was walking home, it was late at night and the moon shone so bright. Everywhere was quiet and peaceful.

I was praying, we had grown up knowing about God.

I was alone and it was really late at night, anybody could have been around. I was praying to God, to get me home safe and talking to Him in my head.

When all of a sudden, I felt this peace, amazing peace came over me. I knew God had heard me, I knew everything was going to be OK. It was so amazing, I remember it like it was yesterday.

We had been brought up in church and Mum took us regularly. So we had always been brought up knowing the bible and studied bible stories in Sunday school.

Mum would buy us kids teaching and worship songs. I still remember some of the songs and words even now. Mum would always listen to worship music, especially on a Sunday when she would invite family over for a yummy roast.

But this was something amazing, something special, something personal. God spoke deep into my heart and gave me a peace that only He could.

John 14 v 27

Peace I leave with you, my peace I give you,
not as the world gives do I give to you.
Let not your heart be troubled, neither let it be afraid. (NKJV)

Chapter 2. The next chapter
Things start to change

So for a while I still went out clubbing at the weekends, taking drugs with my friends. Some different drugs to keep us up all night. I also had some part time cleaning jobs, so I had some money coming in. One weekend we ventured out to Birmingham. This is where I met my first boyfriend. After that, the weekends changed slightly, now I was going over to Birmingham for the weekend. He was a character in himself, not a very nice one, I came to realise as time went on. He was a pretty boy, loved himself and very self involved. His mum and dad were lovely, his mum always looked after me. Our relationship was very volatile, we would argue most of the time. We would spend a lot of time down the pub.

I went to college as I was doing a children rep course. You got a guaranteed interview at the end. I made loads of friends and life changed. College was great fun, I loved it so much, so much better than school. As my boyfriend at the time did not smoke, I eventually cut down and eventually stopped. This was such a blessing, I actually felt like I had my life back. Something good did come out of it.

I had so much fun on my course, we ended up going to Majorca for a week, to help with our studies, as it was a reps course too. It was such fun, I had a great time but the boyfriend was so jealous it was hard to deal with his constant negativity.

At the end of the course I had my interview, I passed I got a job. Wow I was so excited, I was going to work abroad and travel the world. Exciting time.

The boyfriend was not happy, this was so hard. I had worked really hard to get where I was, he was just so miserable. He ended up coming with me. He made out to everyone that he had got a job but it was my job.

Big mistake, he ended up cheating on me and going off with someone else. This was a blessing in disguise but completely broke me. I was heartbroken, my world all of a sudden changed. It was strange being on my own. As this was my first proper boyfriend, it hit me hard.

Away from home, no friend or family to confide in. Hard times. So I ended up getting drunk, partying, meeting different guys. I did start seeing a guy, he was cool. His family came to see him and stayed at our hotel. We looked after their kids. They invited me out with them. As the season was finishing soon, he was planning to go home. We did have some fun nights, me and the girl I worked with. We had a strong friendship and did pretty much everything together. Her mum became ill and she had to leave. I was really lost, my best mate had gone.

I worked away for 3 years, I loved it. I made lots of friends, I made loads of memories good and bad. I was going out meeting new people, looking after children in the sun. I was outgoing and my confidence grew. I lived life my way.

When I came back to the UK. I got a job in a warehouse, with my mum and stepdad. I still went out at weekends. I had a steady boyfriend at that time. I met him in my second season abroad. We were together a few years. I was living back home with my mum and stepdad. It was OK, life just went on.

We went to a church in Kenilworth for years and this is where I got baptised, it was an amazing day. The church was packed with family, church family and friends. What a celebration it was.

Luke 15 v 10

Likewise I say unto you, there is joy in the presence of the angels of God over one sinner who repents.

Mum came back one day and said she met a couple that lived in Bilton and they attended a church there.

Me and mum started going. We attended the Alpha Course, they met once a week. We had a meal, they would talk about God and then you could ask questions. It was a safe space to ask questions. We went for a weekend away, it was amazing. It was there God showed me and revealed to me, what Jesus Christ had done on the cross for me. Jesus went through all that hurt and pain for me. To save me so I could come to the father just as I was.

I was overwhelmed, the tears rolled down my face. I was broken. I had a lot of scars from the past, failed relationships, my dad leaving, drinking, sleeping with different partners, one night stands, etc the list goes on. Things did change small steps at a time, I still went out at the weekends. I split from my boyfriend at the time this was really hard but it was my decision. He had cheated when we first started dating and I just didn't trust him anymore. A few weeks later I was with someone else. Working in the warehouse with all the guys. I fancied one of them and we got on really well. We spent nearly every day together. I got to know him very well. He was so care free and loved life.

I moved to a different job back in childcare.

God really showed himself faithful when life throws some really hard punches. I got accused of things I had not really done at my job. This turned my life upside down. I had my life all planned out and this just turned my world upside down. I had to lean on God. God was there every step of the way and He was faithful throughout the whole mess. I had people at church praying and standing with me. Life carried on for a little longer, then another fatal blow my stepdad got drunk, getting abusive with me and my mum. This ended up with me and him fighting, he cut my face and threw me into the door. The police came and locked him up for the night as he was so drunk. Mum told him to leave the day after. The police eventually took it to court after a lot of we will, we won't. Again God showed himself faithful. He gave me the strength and courage I needed to get through. He was there through it all. I remember praying in the toilets at the court. Lord just let him be found guilty and that day he did.

Mum got baptised, again re-committing her life back to the Lord. A lovely and emotional day. I stood up and did a reading, the church was packed.

Another heartbreak valley, our best mate got bowel cancer, we went to see him in hospital it was heartbreaking. I prayed for his healing, I cried out to God to heal him. Things started to look up he got a lot better. Later on got the all clear from the cancer. This was great news, I praised and thanked God for His healing power. Then after a few months we found out it had come back. Our best mate had been given weeks to live. I struggled with this. I cried out to the Lord with tears. I asked God why my prayers hadn't been answered. I struggled, I didn't understand why? I wrestled with God, were my prayers not heard? Did God not listen. Did I not pray right? Questions and questions. Eventually I realised, I did what I could do and that was pray. The rest was up to God. I had to trust

Him, I had to rely on Him. He was sovereign overall. My faith was shaken. I had to dig in and stand on His word. Even though my world was crumbling. Even though the storms and seas of life were raging. I had to hold on.

I started to understand this verse in:

Proverbs 3 5-6

Trust in the Lord with all your heart, do not depend on your own understanding, seek His will in all you do and He will show you which path to take.

I realised, I needed to let it go and let God be God. I don't need to know all the answers, that's not faith or trust.

My relationship with my current boyfriend also broke down just before this happened. As we were all close friends, I found this very hard. Another valley to walk through things that were changing, I couldn't keep up, I felt my world being shaken. All I could do was hold on to my Saviour, my Lord and my God. To stand on His word and pour my heart out before Him.

Hebrews 13 v 5

Jesus said I never leave you or for sake you.
So we may boldly say: The Lord is my Helper,
I will not fear. What can man do to me?

Chapter 3. The dark days
The danger zone

So the next chapter begins. I was still living life going out and partying, one foot in the church and one foot in the world. I went to church, I knew God but I was also living life how I wanted to and not much changed. One day I went to my friend house, she mentioned she was having a spiritual medium one evening and would I like to go.

So let's stop here a minute. So your all probably cringing at this point and say no don't do it.

The bible says don't mix with these things.

Deuteronomy 18 9-14.

When you come into this land which the Lord your God is giving you, you shall not learn to follow the abominations of those nations. There shall not be found among you, anyone who makes his son or his daughter pass through the fire, or one who practices witchcraft, or a soothsayer, or one who interprets omens, or a sorcerer, or one who conjures spells, or mediums or a spiritist, or one who calls up the dead.

For ALL who do these things are an ABOMINATION to the Lord, and because of these abominations the Lord your God drives them out before you. You shall be blameless before the Lord your God. For these nations which you will dispossess listened to soothsayer and diviner, but as for you, the Lord your God has not appointed such for you.

So we get the picture. Don't go near any witchcraft or mediums, spiritualists and occult practices. I still went. Not only did I go, not long after I started dating this guy. Silly girl and yes I was. I thought he believed in God and yes he did, just not the God I knew the God of the Bible.

We all sin and fall short of the glory of God. We all do life our own way, as we know best. Do we? No we don't, but we all have free will to make our own choices.

It cost me more than I could think or imagine. But at the time I was looking for love, someone who would love me but more importantly love God.

We have all done it, got out of the boat and said do you know what Lord, I got this and off we go and end up in more mess. Yes and that's exactly what I did.

This guy loves God, this is my chance. How silly was I, how little did I know. If I knew now when this started I would of said no thanks and ran to the hills.

So anyway back to the story. I was intrigued by what this guy was saying. We started dating then he started doing my reading and stuff. I started getting interested in the tarot cards, crystals, angels card, horoscopes, star signs. We carried on dating and we moved in together.

I went to tell my friends at church about my new boyfriend. As you can imagine they didn't take the news well. I ended up having a two hour ear bashing. This was my friends looking out for me and voicing their concerns. Did I listen. Of course not, I knew what I was doing. God let me do it as he gives us free will.

I wish I hadn't, I wish I had listened. I didn't.

Things were great at first, then it all changed. It caused division in my family and we moved out together. I look back now and still can't believe what happened and how I acted. We moved into his friend's house, which went from bad to worse. I hated living there it was hell on earth. The darkest place for darkness to dwell. I hated living there but still I stayed. I didn't want my family to think they were right. It still got worse. I can't even explain most of it but it was the worse time of my life. I'd have horrible nightmares of people coming to get us. The devil was having his fun, it was like being on his play ground. I hate it so much, I lived in fear, but still I stayed. This somehow caused more arguments between us. He would come up to bed and start arguing with me, half the time I would not know why. I hate it there, I just wanted to go home. I was so unhappy, I would go to work, I confided in the ladies at work.

What did they think? It was great just to get away, to be out. I remember pulling up outside the house I dreaded going in. I just wanted to drive off, I hated this life. He spent most of my money as he was not working much. This also caused arguments, as I was paying everything. Eventually he told me he couldn't be with me anymore, because of this that and the other. So I moved my stuff out and went to a friend, this also seemed to end in disaster. I stayed a few days and went home. I wanted to be with my family, enough was enough. I lived in this darkness for long enough. We were together a year and what a year it was. Never again.

I packed my things one morning before work and went home. My mum greeted me, I brought all my stuff home. It was good being home but I was still on edge from all the upset. At least it was peaceful no more fear. I even slept better. I had lost loads of weight, I was like a twig. He still kept calling and I kept running. I still had loads of cards, angel cards, crystal, books, Harry Potter and Lord of the rings DVDs, dream catchers. I was still having reading with mediums and spiritualists. I moved into a shared house, we were still on and off.

It was better there and I got on with the people that lived there. What my mum and sister must of thought.

I had a big argument with my landlord and moved out. I went to have a reading she told me someone close was not good for me and I need to say away. I was just about to start a new job. That was the final straw. He was on, off, on and off. He had been leading me on and enough was enough. I text and said I didn't want to hear from him again, it was finished over. I finished it with this guy. I took control of something that felt so out of control. It was for good this time no more. No more contact, no more nothing, it was over and finished enough was enough.

I moved to a village called Church Lawford. It was lovely out in the countryside. The lady had horses out the back and she would let me ride her horse. It was great. Life was so much better, I was a lot happier but I had lots of scars from what had happened. I was angry with my mum and sister as I felt they didn't care. I was the one who withdrew from them. Now I was blaming them, how many times have we done that? Nobody knew about my hurts and scares, they were all inside. I was very damaged. I didn't talk about what happened I kept it inside and wrote in my journal. At least things were looking up.

Romans 8 v 28
And we know that all things work together for the good to them that love God, who are called according to his purpose.

Chapter 4. New beginnings
Change of heart

So here is where the changes really started to happen.

I went to a quiet day, ran by the The Well Christian Healing Centre, at a church in Leamington Spa. I went with my mum. This is the day things changed and God really showed Himself to me, in so many amazing ways. At the quiet day, it's a time for teaching, prayer and reflection. Most importantly a day to spend time with God.

I love going to these days, because of the above. I had not been for a long while.

What happened this day was amazing. They have intervals throughout the day where the well team offer prayer. I put my name down and went for prayer. I went into a room with two ladies and they started to pray. My eyes filled with tears, as I understood how far I had fallen from God. I felt His presence, He was with me and for me. He still loved me no matter what I had done. I cried and cried, I couldn't stop the tears they kept flowing and flowing.

I am welling up even sharing this with you.

When the ladies had finished praying, I shouted out through floods of tears, I had been out with a spiritual medium. One of the ladies said "I was just going to ask you what happened?" The lady looked at me, with a kind and gentle heart. "Tears are healing too." I was sorry for what I had done. I had put someone in the place of God. Not only someone, but someone and somethings that were and are an abomination to my God, and my Jesus who died on the cross for me for my sins. Here I was heartbroken, scared and an emotional wreck. But God still loved me, still had a plan for my life. God had not left me in the pit of darkness or despair. He still loved me.

Even though I had gone off and done life my way. I asked for forgiveness and repented for what I had done.

I had a necklace on that he had bought me, I said I need to get it off. I couldn't do it. I asked the lady to take it off and I threw it in the bin. Gone for ever. I felt this massive weight around my neck lift in Jesus name. The heaviness I had carried for weeks, months, left in seconds. I was free. Free, Free, Free. I felt like a bird being released. When the lady was praying, I had a picture of a bird being released out of it's cage.

So amazing, God stepped down to be with me, to reveal Himself to me. This was the start to a new chapter a new story.

Life changed. I had a good job that I really enjoyed, made new friends. I was a new creation. Something so amazing had happened, God had set me free from the chains that the devil had tried so hard to entangle me in. The devil knows, when you are fully on fire for God that he is in trouble. I stopped drinking and going out so much. I went to church more and made some friends at a church. It was fun, I still didn't feel like it was home. We met up often. Things were changing I was changing.

As I now had a good job and on good money, I decided I wanted my own place. So I moved back in with my mum and started saving. This was the beginning of the year. Me and mum looked at some flats, they were very small. I went into the estate agent for a meeting, when I came out I had a house. It was a lovely two bed house with a garden. A shared ownership property. Perfect, I moved in the September. I have now been here nearly seven years. Amazing. God is so good.

I felt God put on my heart to go to a church in town one Sunday. It was good, a lady sat next to me she was very friendly and we chatted away. Then she left and another lady came. Remember, God had set me free but I still had, all the different cards, tarot cards, angel cards, crystals, books, DVDs, Harry Potter, lord of the ring dvds and other occult items.

This can also include Buddha statues, idols of other gods, dream catches, lucky charms, horoscopes, star signs.

Another lady sat down and we started chatting. She mentioned she was having a teenager Bible group, in her home would I like to go. So I did.

Talk about God's divine appointment, this was

it. She had also been into tarot cards, psychic readings, mediums, fortune tellers, horoscopes and all the rest that comes with it. Wow mind blowing.

We talked and talked, she shared her story and I shared mine. Then she said you need to get rid of all the stuff that's still in your house. I left her house about 11 pm, I got home, I didn't know what I was looking for but God knew. He directed me to where it all was. As soon as I looked in the draw, I knew what it was. Oh how amazing, that night I had a major clear out. The bins were full. As I hadn't been in the house long. I had a neighbour come round and help me put some fittings up. He looked in the bin, I smiled and said I had a clear out.

God had again set me free, from the chains that the devil was still trying to hold me with. The devil will lie to you, keep you in bondage however he can. To stop you knowing the love that God has for you. That's why God sent Jesus, to die on the cross so we can come to Him. Repent, turn from our wicked ways and turn back to Him, and He will set us free.

John 8-36

Therefore if the Son (Jesus) makes you free, you are free indeed.

This is wonderful. Thank you Jesus.

2 Corinthians 2. 15-16

For we are to God the pleasing aroma of

*Christ among those who are being saved
and those who are perishing.*

*To the one we are an aroma that brings
death, to the other, an aroma that brings
life. And who is equal to such a task.*

John 10. 9-10

*Jesus says, "I am the gate, whoever enters
through me will be saved.*

*They will come in and go out and find
pastures.*

*The THIEF (devil) comes ONLY TO STEAL,
KILL AND DESTROY, I have come (Jesus)
that they may have life, and have it to the
full."*

If you want to find out more about the occult
Derek Prince is a great Bible teacher and had an
amazing healing and teaching ministry in this
area.

Ephesians 6 v 10 – 17

*Finally, my brethren, be strong in the Lord
and in the power of his might. Put on
the whole armour of God, that you may
be able to stand against the wiles of the
devil. For we do not wrestle against flesh
and blood, but against the principalities,
against powers, against the rulers of
darkness of this age, against spiritual
hosts of wickedness in the heavenly
places. Therefore take up the whole
armour of God, that you may be able to*

withstand in the evil days, and having done all, to stand.

Stand therefore, having girded your waist with truth, having put on the breastplate of righteousness, and having shod your feet with the preparation of the gospel of peace, above all, take the shield of faith with which you will be able to quench all the fiery darts of the wicked one. And take the helmet of salvation, the sword of the spirit, which is the word of God.

Chapter 5. The last chapter
The journey with Jesus

My journey with Jesus. Jesus gives me access to my Father in heaven. Through what Jesus did on the cross.

Hebrews 4 v 16

Let us therefore come boldly to the throne of grace, that we may obtain mercy and find grace to help in times of need.

What a lovely Bible verse. Its not just when we need help, we can come every day, day after day, after day.

Praise God for Jesus and God's Holy Spirit that changes us. You can read more about Jesus and his ministry in the new testament of the Bible. Matthew, Mark, Luke and John some good bibles are the NIV – New International Version, NLT- New Living Translation or KJV- King James Version.

As I started to seek God more. God showed me a story in the bible about Moses. Moses was a man of God, you can read about him in:

Exodus chapter 1 v12.

He went before the King of Egypt to let the people of Israel go, as they had been slaves in the land. God send plagues to show His power but the Egyptian also used magicians and God showed me through this story His power and might.

Exodus 8 v 18-19

Pharaoh's magicians tried to do the same thing with their secret arts, but this time they failed.

"This must be the finger of God!" The magicians exclaimed to Pharaoh.

God has been so faithful to me. So I moved into my house. It was such a blessing.

We started to go to Renewal Church in Solihull with some friends on a Tuesday evening. I felt like God wanted me to go, so I went before and after work when I could. I remember I was stood in Renewal one Sunday on my own. I had gone before work. I had this feeling come over me like never before. This was home, this is where I need to be. I didn't know anybody but it was home. Not long after I felt God say join and become a member, so I did.

A few months after, I went out with a friend and she invited a guy friend. He was nice looking, lovely eyes and smile. I didn't really give it much thought, we became friend on Facebook. A few months later he asked me out, so we went out. We dated for a while then, we had weekends away. To spend more time getting to know each other. This was challenging for me as this time it was God's way or no way. God was first in my life and I had to obey His word. God showed me how much He loved me, if God loved me that much I wasn't going to settle for anything less. There was no room to compromise.

God says in:

Genesis 2 v 24
Therefore a man shall leave his father and mother and be joined to his wife, and they shall become one flesh.

The Bible is very clear in what it says. We can interpret it how we want or try and dress it up how we want.

I did this for years to justify my sin, but no more this was it. I was all in, no matter the cost.

1 Corinthians 6 v 19
Do you not know that your bodies are the temple of the Holy Spirit, who is in you, whom you have received from God. You are not your own.

The only spirit we should be inviting in our lives is God's Holy Spirt, that brings peace, joy, patience, kindness, love. No more sleeping with anyone outside of marriage. God showed me in this time what marriage meant to Him and how important it was.

I had to honour my God. We did, I can say, we stood on our wedding day pure before a Holy God. We waited for our wedding day. Kevin proposed just after Christmas the first weekend in January in Hull. What an amazing and blessed day it was. God was so in it. We went to town and picked my engagement ring together. It was hard as my mum and sister didn't know, so we told them when we got back on the Sunday. I felt God gave me the 16th of April, I also prayed God would choose who he wanted to marry us. God did. We went to church and got our date 16th April.

Time to plan. God was so good. I tried to book a venue but it was booked. I heard that small voice say ring and I did. The lady on the phone said "I am sorry that room is taken," then she said "wait a minute" she came back and said "we can move the other party into the big room and you can have the smaller room."

Amazing, God was so good. We got married on 16th April 2016. We have now been married 4 years. The best part of being married is we share the same faith. We get to go to church together, praise God together, worship pray and seek the Lord's will for our lives. What a blessing He is. Life has changed so much from the beginning of this book. God is so good.

You can accept Jesus as your Lord and Saviour. Ask for His forgiveness and turn away from you sin into a new fulfilled life in Jesus Christ. All you have to do is say Yes. Open your heart invite Him in and ask Him to change your heart. He will.

God loves us so much that he sent Jesus to die on the cross for you and for me. As it was the only way to rebuild the gap to Our Father in heaven.

The Lord's prayer – **Mathew 6 v 6-13** is a

great place to start. Life may not always be easy but Jesus will walk every step with us. He is our anchor in all storms, draw close to Him and He will draw close to you. Jesus says I will never leave you or forsake you.

2 Corinthians 1 v 3-4

Praise be to the God and Father of our Lord Jesus Christ,

The Father of compassion and the God of all comfort, who comforts us in All Our troubles, so that we can comfort those in any trouble with the comfort we ourselves receive from God.

Thank you

Thank you for reading and sharing my journey.

I hope this has spoken to you and helped you in your Own life journey.

God is so good and accepting Jesus in my life has changed my world. I love Him so much and thank Him each day for what He has done.

Life isn't always easy but Jesus is always near.

And when the storms of life rage He is right beside us.

Whispering words of courage and strength.

Read your Bible stand on the word of God and His promises. Ask Him for a verse to stand on read it every day. I pray this over you.

Numbers 6 v 24-26
The Lord bless you and keep you,
The Lord make His face shine upon you
and be gracious to you and give you peace.

A friend gave me this verse that God gave her when she was praying for me. So I pray this over this book.

Matthew 14 v 21
Go feed the five thousand. I pray it does in
the mighty name of Jesus. Amen.

Lightning Source UK Ltd.
Milton Keynes UK
UKHW050722020822
406716UK00005B/101